MELODIOUS DOUBLE-STOPS

(Mélodies en Doubles-Cordes)

For Violin

By

JOSEPHINE TROTT

Ed. 1594

G. SCHIRMER, *Inc.*

DISTRIBUTED BY

HAL•LEONARD®
CORPORATION

7777 W. BLUEMOUND RD. P.O. BOX 13819 MILWAUKEE, WI 53213

Melodious Double-Stops

Mélodies en Doubles-Cordes

In the first eight exercises one of the two notes is invariably an open string.

Dans les huit premièrs exercices, une des deux notes est toujours une corde à vide.

Do not lift fingers until necessary.
Ne pas lever les doigts sans nécessité.

Josephine Trott

3

Moderato

4

Allegretto

5

Lamentoso

6

Scherzando

10

6

Vigoroso

11

pizz. *l.h.*
m.g.

Commodo

12

rit. - - - -

13 Moderato con moto

14 Andante

20 Moderato

21 Lento

22 Allegretto

Vigoroso

27

Con grazia

28

19

* +⁼ left hand pizzicato.
la main gauche pizz.

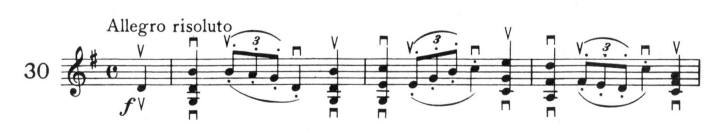

SCHIRMER'S LIBRARY
of Musical Classics

VIOLIN AND PIANO
SERIES TWO

G. SCHIRMER, Inc.   DISTRIBUTED BY   Hal•Leonard®

A-1201

SCHIRMER'S LIBRARY
of Musical Classics
METHODS, STUDIES, EXERCISES AND PIECES
FOR VIOLIN SOLO
SERIES ONE

ALARD, D.

L. 1389 Op. 41. 24 Etude-Caprices (Lichtenerg).

BACH, J. S.

L. 221 6 Sonatas (Herrmann)

BERIOT, C. de

L. 1658 Op. 123. The First 30 Concert Studies (Berkley).

L. 1086 Método para Aprender el Violin (Lehmann). sp. Bk. I

BLUMENSTENGEL, A.

L. 1032 Op. 33. 24 Studies.

L. 603 Scale and Arpeggio Studies. Bk. I: 1st Position.

L. 604 Bk. II: First 3 Positions.

BOHMER, C.

L. 1622 Op. 54. 75 Studies in Intonation (Schill).

CASORTI, A.

L. 932 Op. 50. The Technics of Bowing.

DANCLA, C.

L. 602 Op. 68. 15 Studies. With accompaniment of a 2d Violin.

L. 626 Op. 73. 20 Brilliant and Characteristic Etudes.

L. 219 Op. 74. School of Mechanism. 50 Daily Exercises.

DAVID, F.

L. 1410 Violin Harmonics and the Pizzicato (Smith). sp. e.

DONT, J.

L. 1179 Op. 35. 24 Etudes and Caprices (Berkley).

L. 328 Op. 37. 24 Exercises. Preparatory to the Studies of R. Kreutzer and P. Rode.

L. 429 Op. 38. 30 Progressive Exercises. With accompaniment of a 2d Violin.

ERNST, H. W.

L. 1470 6 Etudes. In Two- to Four-Part Harmony (Auer).

FIORILLO, F.

L. 228 36 Studies or Caprices (Schradieck).

GAVINES, P.

L. 929 24 Studies (Matinées) (Lichtenberg).

GRUNWALD, A.

L. 1390 First Exercises (Svečenski). sp. e.

HERMANN, F.

L. 952 Op. 20. 100 Violin Studies for Beginners (Mittell). sp. e. Bk. I: For the Beginning of Tuition; L. 953, Bk. II: For the Development of Finger- and Bow-Technics.

L. 742 Violin School. Part I. L. 743, Part II.

HOFMANN, R.

L. 863 Op. 25. First Studies. In the First Position. Bk. I: The Beginner; L. 864, Bk. II: The Progressive Pupil; L. 865, Book III: The More Advanced Student.

HRIMALY, J.

L. 842 Scale-Studies.

KAYSER, H. E.

L. 750 Op. 20. 36 Elementary and Progressive Studies (Svečenski). Complete.

The same. L. 306, Bk. I; L. 307, Bk. II; L. 308, Bk. III.

L. 867 Op. 67. The Study of the Positions. 34 Short Pieces.

KREUTZER, R.

L. 230 42 Studies or Caprices (Singer).

G. SCHIRMER, Inc.

DISTRIBUTED BY
HAL•LEONARD®

A-1195

U.S. $9.99

ISBN 978-0-7935-2599-7

G. SCHIRMER, Inc.

HL50327290